Usborne Sp

ROCKS &
MINERALS

Alan Woolley

Photography by Mike Freeman

Illustrated by Cristina Adami, Jeremy Gower,
Ian Jackson, Luis Rey, Chris Shields, Stuart Trotter

Edited by Fiona Watt, Gill Harvey, Rosemary Hartill and Sue Jacquemier
Geological advisor : Annette Shelford
Designed by Cristina Adami
Series editor : Philippa Wingate
Cover designer: Joanne Kirkby
Series designer : Laura Fearn
US editors: Erwin King and Carrie Armstrong

Picture credits : Cover: © blickwinkel/Alamy. Title page: ©Corbis/Gary Thomas
Sutto. Pages 4-5: Corbis/Tom Bean. Page 43 (Rhyolite): ©The Natural History
Museum, London. Backgrounds on pages 1–3 and 6–64: © Digital Vision.

This edition first published in 2006 by Usborne Publishing Ltd., Usborne House,
83-85 Saffron Hill, London, EC1N 8RT, England. www.usborne.com.
First published in America in 2006.

CONTENTS

HOW TO USE THIS BOOK

This book is an identification guide to many types of minerals, rocks and fossils. It begins by explaining the difference between these three categories, how they are formed, and what the Earth is made of. Descriptions of the individual specimens are arranged with minerals first, rocks next and fossils last.

Each specimen has a photograph and a description to help you identify it. There is also a circle to mark if you spot it

USEFUL WORDS AND SCORECARD

On page 60, there is a list explaining some of the more difficult words that appear in this book.

The scorecard on pages 62 and 63 gives you a score for each mineral, rock, or fossil you spot.

WHERE TO LOOK

The rocks, minerals and fossils in this book are from all around the world, so a good place to spot them is at a natural history or geological museum.

Many of them occur naturally in North America, so look around you when you are out in the country or walking along a beach.

Another good place to look is in towns, as many buildings are built out of rock. Look in gift shops, too – some sell polished or unpolished minerals and fossils, while others sell jewelry set with different stones. You may also see some interesting examples if you visit tourist attractions, such as underground caves.

These amazing rocks are made up of layers of sandstone.

STUDYING THE EARTH

The Earth is made up of several layers. The solid outer layer, known as the crust, is relatively thin. It is made up of three different kinds of rocks: igneous, sedimentary and metamorphic. You can find out about these on pages 9-13. The middle layer of the Earth is called the mantle. The central part of the Earth is called the core.

Geologists (scientists who study the Earth and what it is made of) can find out quite easily about the rocks in the crust. They collect samples from the surface and drill into the crust to collect rocks from deeper down.

This picture of the Earth has been cut away to show its layers (not to scale).

Throughout this book, you will find suggested links to rocks and minerals websites. For a complete list of links and instructions, turn to page 61.

It's more difficult to find out about the mantle and the core. Clues about them come from volcanic eruptions which bring molten or melted rock from the mantle to the surface.

Geologists also discover things about the layers by looking at the way earthquake shock waves travel through the Earth.

THE CRUST
is between 3 miles (5km) and 43 miles (70km) thick, and is made up of different types of rock.

THE MANTLE
is about 1,900 miles (3,000km) thick. It is made of silicon and magnesium. The top and lower parts are solid rock. The middle part has melted to form a substance called magma.

THE CORE
is probably made of iron and nickel. The outer core is about 1,400 miles (2,200km) thick and is melted rock, whereas the inner core is solid. It is about 800 miles (1,300km) thick.

Outer core

Inner core

WHAT ARE MINERALS?

Minerals occur naturally in the Earth, and are the chemical substances that rocks are made of. Minerals, in turn, are made of "elements" – simple substances that cannot be broken down into any other substance. Some minerals, such as gold, are made of only one element, but most are made of two or more.

Granite is a rock made from a mixture of minerals, mainly feldspar, quartz and mica.

The mineral hematite sometimes forms rounded lumps.

RECOGNIZING MINERALS

Many minerals have a particular shape or color that will help you to identify them. Some form crystals with flat surfaces and regular shapes. Others are found as shapeless lumps or "masses." Some also form crusts on other rocks and minerals.

Amethyst crystals

Smithsonite forms crusts on other rocks.

WHAT ARE ROCKS?

Rocks are usually made up
of a mixture of different kinds
of minerals. There are three
types of rocks: igneous,
sedimentary and
metamorphic. These are
formed in different ways.

This diagram shows
where the three
different kinds of
rocks are formed.

Sedimentary
rocks form on seabeds,
rivers and lakes.

Igneous rocks are
formed from magma
(see pages 10-11)

Metamorphic
rocks are
formed when
they are
heated or
crushed by
igneous rocks
nearby.

IGNEOUS ROCKS

There are two kinds of igneous rock, extrusive and intrusive. They are formed in different ways. Beneath the Earth's crust lies red-hot molten rock, called magma. Magma is a mushy liquid, made up of a mixture of different melted minerals and mineral crystals.

The picture below shows molten lava oozing from a volcano.

During a volcanic eruption magma is forced through a weakness in the Earth's crust onto the surface. It cools and solidifies to form rock. When magma is forced onto the Earth's surface, it is known as lava. Rocks formed in this way are called extrusive igneous rocks.

For a link to a fun online introduction to Earth science, turn to page 61.

Other kinds of igneous rocks are formed when magma works its way in between layers of rocks and solidifies before it reaches the surface. These are called intrusive igneous rocks.

Intrusive igneous rocks may appear on the Earth's surface if the overlying rocks are worn away.

This diagram shows a batholith, the largest kind of intrusive igneous rock.

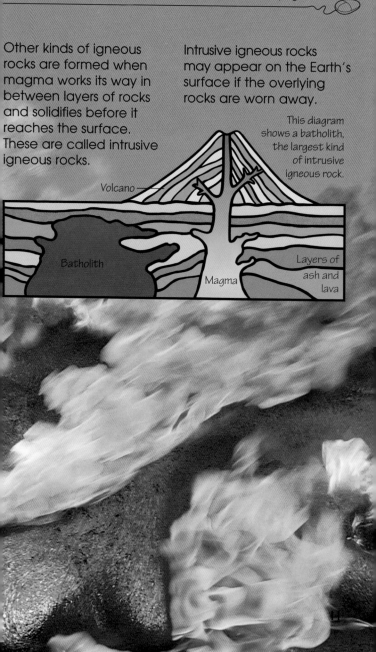

Volcano

Batholith

Magma

Layers of ash and lava

SEDIMENTARY ROCKS

Sedimentary rocks are made from fragments of rocks and the remains of animals and plants.

Rain, wind and ice wear away tiny pieces of rock from exposed surfaces, such as these mountains. The fragments are called sediment.

Rain washes the sediment into rivers or streams. The fragments tumble and knock against each other. This grinds them down to form sand and mud. Eventually the sediment is washed into the sea.

On the seabed, the sediment builds up in layers along with the remains of sea creatures. In time, the layers are packed down by the weight of the layers on top. Over millions of years, they become solid rock.

METAMORPHIC ROCKS

Metamorphic rocks are formed
when sedimentary or igneous rocks
are altered by high temperatures
or pressure, or both. The heat
and pressure change the texture,
appearance and chemical
composition of the rocks.

Marble is a
metamorphic
rock formed from
limestone.

When magma comes
into contact with other
rocks, these rocks become
metamorphic rocks.

Metamorphic
rocks

Sedimentary
rocks

Magma

➡ Some metamorphic
rocks are formed when
magma is forced into
an area of the Earth's
crust. The magma
heats the surrounding
rocks, changing
their composition.

When two plates
move together, all the
rocks between them are
crushed and squeezed.

➡ Although the Earth's
crust appears to be solid,
it is actually broken into
several enormous
pieces, called plates.
These plates are
constantly moving at a
rate of about 2 inches
(50mm) each year. This
builds up pressure in the
crust, causing rocks to change

WHAT ARE FOSSILS?

Fossils are the impressions or remains of animals and plants that have been preserved in rocks (usually sedimentary rocks). When animals and plants die, they often decay or are eaten. Fossils form when they are covered with sand or mud (sediment) before they decay.

Fossils are formed in two ways. They can consist o the actual material of a plant or animal that has been preserved, such as shells or bones; or they can be formed from minerals that filled the space left behind when the animal or plant dissolved away.

1. Millions of years ago ichthyosaurs, like these, lived in the sea.

2. When an ichthyosaur died, its remains sank to the seabed.

3. The soft body decayed, but the skeleton was covered in sediment and preserved. The bones were slowly replaced by minerals, and a fossil formed.

14

For a link to a website about periods of geologic time, turn to page 61.

Remains of animals that are now extinct have also been found preserved in things other than rocks. In northern Siberia, mammoths have been found preserved in ice. The ice acts like a giant freezer.

Mammoths were larger than elephants and were covered in a hairy coat.

Some fossils, known as trace fossils, are the remains of marks, such as footprints or burrows.

This fossil shows burrows made by tiny worms that lived on the bed of a shallow sea.

Fossils of dinosaur footprints may show details of the skin and deep imprints of the claws.

Whole insects can be found preserved in amber. These insects were trapped in resin which dripped from trees. The resin hardened, leaving the insect inside.

An insect preserved in amber

15

MINERALS

← **GOLD**
Gold is a metal, and an unmixed element. It is usually found as tiny yellow specks, but occasionally forms larger lumps called "nuggets." It occurs in igneous and sedimentary rocks, and is sometimes found in river sand and gravel. It is softer than "fool's gold" (pyrite or chalcopyrite – see pages 17-18).

Because gold is rare, it is considered a symbol of power and wealth.

Flecks of gold glisten in this piece of rock.

➡ **SILVER**
Silver can be found as small specks and also as wiry shapes. It usually occurs in igneous rocks. It is silver-white, but quickly tarnishes (goes dull and black) when exposed to air. Silver, like gold, is one of the few metals that is found unmixed with other elements.

← SULFUR

Another unmixed element, found in rocks near volcanoes and around hot springs. It usually makes a powdery crust on rocks, but can also form large crystals. It burns easily, with a strong, unpleasant smell. It is usually bright yellow, but can be brownish.

→ PYRITE

Pyrite is a common mineral, made of iron and sulfur. It is also called iron pyrites, or fool's gold, because of its pale brassy-yellow color. It is actually a paler yellow than real gold. Many fossils are made of pyrite. It forms crystals, particularly cube-shaped ones. It also forms nodules (rounded lumps) in some rocks, such as shale and chalk.

A single cube-shaped pyrite crystal

17

MINERALS

← CHALCOPYRITE
Chalcopyrite is sometimes called copper pyrites and, like pyrite, is also known as fool's gold. It is made of the elements copper, iron and sulfur, and is found in a wide range of metamorphic and igneous rocks. It forms irregular lumps, and sometimes crystals. It is brass-yellow, but will tarnish and look iridescent (how oil looks on water, with shimmering reds, blues and purples).

→ GALENA
Galena is made of the elements lead and sulfur. It often forms cube-shaped crystals. It is found in some sedimentary rocks, and often with pyrite, sphalerite, and chalcopyrite. When it is freshly split it is a shining silver-gray, but it tarnishes to dull gray with time.

➡ SPHALERITE

Sphalerite is also known as zinc blende, blende or black jack. It often occurs with galena and can easily be mistaken for other minerals. It varies from brown to black, but can be yellow and sometimes transparent. It is the source of most of the world's zinc.

⬅ ARSENOPYRITE

Arsenopyrite also has the strange name of mispickel. It is made of sulfur, iron and arsenic, and is often found with gold and quartz. It may form crystals. Arsenopyrite is silver to grayish-white, and may have a brownish tarnish.

MINERALS

➡ GRAPHITE

Graphite is made of the element carbon. It is often found in schist, a kind of metamorphic rock, and limestone, a sedimentary rock, most commonly as tiny grains but sometimes as flat crystals. The name comes from the Greek word *graphos*, which means "to write."

The "lead" in pencils is not lead at all, but a mixture of clay and graphite.

⬇ DIAMOND

Like graphite, diamond is made of carbon. It occurs mainly in a rock called kimberlite. Not all diamonds are clear – they can be yellow, red, black or brown. It is the hardest mineral known.

Natural diamonds do not sparkle. They only sparkle when they are cut and light shines through them.

➡ CORUNDUM

This mineral is made of aluminum and oxygen. It is found mainly in metamorphic rocks. It forms crystals of different shapes. These can be brown, yellow or green, but the best-known kinds are red and blue (see below). Corundum is very hard and is used to make the rough surface on emery boards and sandpaper.

Uncut
ruby

Rubies

Sapphire

⬅ SAPPHIRE and RUBY

These are varieties of corundum. Sapphire is pale blue and transparent, while ruby is pink to blood-red and is also transparent. Together with diamonds and emeralds, these are the most precious gemstones.

21

MINERALS

Goethite often forms
rounded lumps or long,
sausage-like masses.
It is called a secondary
mineral, which means a
mineral that is formed by
the alteration of other
minerals. Goethite is
nearly always formed
by the effect of
water on minerals
such as magnetite
and pyrite. It is usually
very dark brown, but
may be yellow-brown.

→ PYROLUSITE
Pyrolusite is made
of manganese and
oxygen. It often forms
fern-like shapes in
sedimentary rocks.
These are called
dendrites and are
often mistaken for
fossil leaves. It also
forms masses of thin
crystals. Large crystals
are rare. Nodules (rounded
lumps) of pyrolusite are
found on the seabed.

Halite crystals

← HALITE

Halite is also called "rock salt," but it is best known as the table salt you eat. It was formed thousands of years ago by the evaporation of sea water. Thick layers of it are found in sedimentary rock.

Halite is usually found in masses (see page 8), but it can also be found as single, cube-shaped crystals. It is transparent or white in its purest form, but is usually stained brown or yellow.

→ FLUORITE

Fluorite is also called fluorspar. It forms cube-shaped crystals that are often blue, violet, purple, green or yellow, though white or pink types are sometimes found, too. In ultraviolet light, it glows with an effect called fluorescence, which is named after fluorite.

MINERALS

➤ CALCITE

Calcite is made of calcium, carbon and oxygen. It is usually white, but can be gray, green, yellow, red or blue. When it is broken, it forms six-sided shapes, called rhombs. This is the mineral that forms "fur" inside kettles.

Crystalline calcite

Dogstooth calcite

Iceland spar. Anything looked at through this type of calcite appears as double.

Limestone and marble are made mostly of calcite. Stalactites and stalagmite (see page 48) are formed when water containing a type of calcite drips from the roof of a cave in limestone areas.

24

For a link to an interactive site about gems and minerals, turn to page 61.

◀ MALACHITE
Malachite is made of copper, carbon, oxygen and hydrogen. The copper gives it its color – it is bright green with bands of lighter and darker shades of green. The bands can be clearly seen when it is cut and polished. It is often used in jewelry.

A piece of polished malachite, showing the banded patterns

➡ SMITHSONITE
Smithsonite is made of zinc, carbon and oxygen. It can be white, gray, green, blue, yellow, purple or brown. Its tiny crystals form bubbly looking rounded masses. It also forms crusts, coating other minerals and rocks.

25

MINERALS

◀ BARITE

Crystals of barite are quite common. They tend to be white, but may be tinged with yellow, brown or red. Barite is often glassy-looking and transparent, and is often found in the holes between layers of limestone. It contains the element barium, which gives the bright-green color in flares and fireworks.

➡ GYPSUM

Gypsum is generally white, but may be shades of gray, yellow or pink. It sometimes forms clear crystals, called selenite. You may see it as alabaster, a fine-grained form of gypsum that is carved into ornaments, bowls and other objects.

➡ APATITE

Your teeth are made mostly of apatite, and so are your bones. A sedimentary rock called phosphate rock is made almost entirely of apatite, and is mined for use as a fertilizer. Pure apatite is made mainly of calcium and phosphorus, and may be pale green, blue-green, white or brown.

Apatite crystals

A polished piece of turquoise

⬅ TURQUOISE

Turquoise is made mainly of copper, aluminum and phosphorus. Its color varies from sky-blue to apple-green, which makes it popular as a gemstone. It is usually found in hot, dry regions as masses or as a crust. Crystals are small and very rare.

MINERALS

An uncut
garnet

← GARNET
Garnet is a mixture of
several elements, and
there are many different
kinds. It forms crystals,
which are often dark red
and red-brown, but can
also be green. They are
common in some
metamorphic rocks.
Garnets are frequently
used to make jewelry.

A cut and
polished garnet

➡ TOURMALINE
Tourmaline forms long
crystals which have
parallel lines running
along their length. If you
look at right angles to
these lines, you will see
that they form a roughly
triangular shape.
Tourmaline is often black,
but blue, pink and green
crystals also occur.

➡ OLIVINE

Olivine is made of magnesium, iron, silicon and oxygen. It usually forms grainy masses. It is often olive-green, but some kinds are white and others black. When it is green and transparent it is called peridot, and may be used as a gemstone.

⬅ SERPENTINE

Serpentine is a common mineral that is usually green, but may be yellow or gray. It can be striped or speckled. It is found as irregular lumps, or as thin fibers, like pieces of cotton. These fibers are known as asbestos. The dust from asbestos is very bad for your health.

MINERALS

➤ BERYL

Beryl is made of the elements silicon, oxygen, aluminum and beryllium. It usually forms long crystals with six sides. Transparent beryl is known by different names. As well as aquamarine and emerald (see below), there is a yellow type called heliodor and a pink type called morganite.

◄ EMERALD and AQUAMARINE

These are varieties of beryl. Emerald is a transparent dark-green or light-green gemstone, most commonly found in Colombia. Aquamarine is the name for pale blue-green beryl. Emerald is rarer than aquamarine, and therefore, a much more valuable gemstone.

Emerald

Aquamarine

➡ AUGITE

Augite is made up mainly of calcium, magnesium, aluminum, iron and silicon. It forms short, fat column-shaped crystals with eight sides. In color, it ranges from black to dark green. Augite is principally found in basalts and other types of igneous rocks.

⬅ HORNBLENDE

Hornblende is made up of a wide variety of elements. It forms fairly large crystals. These are column-shaped, and can be short or long. They vary from green to black. Hornblende is found in a wide range of igneous and metamorphic rocks, and forms a large part of a rock called amphibolite.

MINERALS

➡ MICA

There are two main kinds of mica – biotite is black or brown and shiny, and muscovite is white and silvery. Both are made up of thin sheets or flakes. When separated, these layers are so thin they are transparent. Both types are common in granites, pegmatites and schists (different kinds of igneous and metamorphic rocks).

Biotite

Muscovite

⬅ TALC

Talc is made of silicon, magnesium, oxygen and hydrogen. It is the softest mineral known. You can scratch it easily with a fingernail. It is usually pale green, but may be white or gray. Talc is used to make talcum powder. Some rocks, called soapstone or steatite, are made almost entirely of talc.

QUARTZ

Quartz is made of silicon and oxygen. It is found in igneous, sedimentary and metamorphic rocks. There are many varieties, some of which are described over the next few pages. The crystals are usually six-sided, and can be found in a range of different colors.

Rock crystal

Milky quartz

Shapes of some perfect quartz crystals

⬆ MILKY QUARTZ and ROCK CRYSTAL

The most common variety of quartz is the opaque, white kind, called milky quartz. Clear transparent quartz is called rock crystal and is sometimes mistaken for diamonds. It is found as crystals or small irregular lumps.

33

or a link to games to test your mineral knowledge, turn to page 61.

MINERALS

➡ AMETHYST

Amethyst is another type of quartz. It is transparent and varies in color from deep purple to pale blue. It is popular as a semi-precious stone and is often set in jewelry. It forms crystals that can be found as crusts lining holes in volcanic rocks.

⬅ SMOKY QUARTZ

Smoky quartz forms transparent to translucent crystals, with six sides. They range from smoky-brown to nearly black in color. Smoky quartz is sometimes known as cairngorm, after the Cairngorm mountains in Scotland where it is found

◀ CHALCEDONY

This is another variety of quartz. It is very fine-grained and does not form crystals, usually forming rounded masses instead. There are many varieties of chalcedony (see below). It varies from white to gray, but may also be red, brown or black.

➡ TYPES OF CHALCEDONY

Different kinds of chalcedony include carnelian, sard, jasper, chrysoprase and heliotrope, all of which are used in jewelry. Carnelian and sard are red or reddish brown. Jasper is opaque and usually dark red, but may be yellow or brown. Chrysoprase is apple-green, while heliotrope or "bloodstone" is green with red spots that look like blood.

A polished piece of carnelian

MINERALS

➡ AGATE

Agate is a kind of quartz made up of many colored bands. Most agate occurs in rounded lumps, which vary from the size of a marble to that of a football. The middle of the agate may consist of rock crystal. The bands vary from milky white to green, brown, red and black. If the bands are straight, it is called onyx.

⬅ OPAL

Opal is made of silicon, oxygen and water. It varies in color from clear to translucent milky white, gray, blue, green, red, brown or black. Precious opal often has a variety of iridescent blues, reds and yellows. In fire opal, red and yellow colors make fire-like reflections. Opal is often polished and set in jewelry.

A polished
piece of opal

◄ ORTHOCLASE FELDSPAR

Feldspars are minerals made up of a variety of elements, and they form a large part of igneous rocks. Orthoclase feldspar forms stubby four- and six-sided crystals that range in color from milky white to pale pink. The white or pink grains that you see in polished granite are usually orthoclase.

➤ PLAGIOCLASE FELDSPAR

Plagioclase feldspar can form flat crystals, but it is much more commonly found as an irregular mass. It occurs in a wide range of igneous rocks. One type, called labradorite, is often striking in color with a variety of iridescent blues and greens.

Labradorite, a type of plagioclase feldspar

MINERALS

◄ MAGNETITE
Magnetite is made of
iron and oxygen. It forms
black crystals, the same
shape as natural
diamond crystals
(see page 20).
It is strongly
magnetic, so if
you put it near
a compass it
will make the
needle move.

► HEMATITE
Like magnetite, hematite
is made of iron and
oxygen, but in different
proportions.
Hematite is
named after the
Greek word for
blood, as it often
ranges from dull to
bright red, but it
can be steel-gray
or black. It is also
known as kidney
ore because of its
shape. It is often found
in sedimentary rocks,

38

IGNEOUS ROCKS

◀ TUFF

Tuff is made up from small pieces of volcanic rock and crystals cemented together into hard rock. It is built up, layer by layer, from the ash formed by a succession of volcanic explosions. In coarse-grained tuffs, you can see the individual rounded pieces of rock, together with broken crystals of minerals.

➡ AGGLOMERATE

This is made of large lumps of volcanic rock, such as basalt, which have been thrown out of a volcano by violent eruptions. The lumps are at least 2½ inches (6cm) across, and can be many yards wide. They may be pieces of rock from inside a volcano, or "bombs" – pieces of lava which have cooled as they were hurled through the air.

Some volcanic bombs form a "tail" as they twist through the air.

IGNEOUS ROCKS

← GRANITE
Granite is a coarse-grained igneous rock. It can be white, gray or pink, and is usually spotted because of the different minerals it contains. The main minerals are feldspar, quartz and mica. Granite is often polished, then used as a decorative building stone.

➡ PEGMATITE
This is a very coarse rock which contains large crystals. The main minerals are feldspar, quartz and mica (particularly muscovite), but there may be hundreds of others too. Because the crystals in pegmatites are so large, they are some of the best rocks for studying lots of different minerals.

➡ GABBRO

This is a coarse-grained rock with an even texture. It is usually greenish dark gray or black, and is often speckled with minerals, such as plagioclase feldspar, augite and olivine. It is an extrusive igneous rock (see pages 10-11) that has cooled slowly, allowing large crystals to grow.

⬅ SERPENTINITE

This is made mainly of the mineral serpentine. It is often patchy, streaky and veined, with tiny fibers of serpentine running across the veins. It is usually dark green, but may have black, white or even red patches and streaks. Surfaces that are exposed to the weather may be red-brown.

IGNEOUS ROCKS

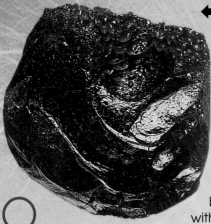

◀ OBSIDIAN
Obsidian is natural glass, formed when magma from a volcano cools very rapidly. It cools so quickly that crystals rarely have time to form. It is usually shiny and black, but can be gray or red-brown. Obsidian breaks easily into pieces with sharp edges and smooth, rounded surfaces.

➡ PUMICE
Pumice is full of tiny gas bubbles, so it is very light and will often float on water. It tends to be gray, but may be yellowish. Pumice is formed when magma containing bubbles of gas reaches the Earth's surface. Then, if the magma cools quickly, the bubbles are preserved in the rock. Pumice is often used as an abrasive for making things smooth.

➡ RHYOLITE

Rhyolite is similar to granite, but has finer grains. It may contain a few large crystals of feldspar or quartz. It is white or gray, but can also be reddish or black. It may also have bands running through it. These were caused by layers of lava flowing from a volcano.

⬅ BASALT

This is a fine- to medium-grained rock that ranges in color from black to dark gray. It is volcanic, and may form lava flows that cover huge areas. It also builds up to form volcanoes. When thick flows of basalt lava cool down, they often break into six-sided columns.

SEDIMENTARY ROCKS

Sandstone

Ripple marks on a slab of sandstone

Grit

⬆ SANDSTONE and GRIT

Sandstone and grit are made of grains of sand held together usually by calcite or a substance called silica. The grains are often quartz, but can be feldspar or other minerals. If the grains are angular, rather than smooth and round, the rock is called a grit. The color of both sandstone and grit may be yellow, red, white or greenish, depending on where they were formed. Most deposits of sand were formed in the sea, carried there by rivers. For this reason, ripple marks, like those seen on sandy beaches when the tide goes out, are quite commonly found in sandstones. Sandstone is also found in deserts. It is formed from sand blown there by the wind. This type of sandstone is usually red.

For a link to a site with information on rock collecting, turn to page 61.

➡ SILTSTONE

Siltstone is formed from compacted "silt." Silt is sediment which is finer-grained than sand but coarser than mud. Sometimes you can see the glint of tiny mica flakes in it, or larger grains of feldspar or quartz. It is often pale to dark gray in color. Fossils are common in siltstone.

⬅ MUDSTONE and SHALE

These rocks are formed from the hardening of fine mud in the sea. If the rock has many fine layers, it is called shale; if not, it is called mudstone. Both are often black to dark gray in color, but may be brown, red or green. They often contain fossils, which are preserved as the mineral pyrite.

45

SEDIMENTARY ROCKS

Limestone containing fossils of shells

➡ LIMESTONE

Limestone is a common sedimentary rock made up mainly of the mineral calcite. The calcite may have very fine grains, or it may form crystals ½ inch (10mm) or more across. It is often layered, though the layers can be hard to spot.

Limestone is often grayish white in color, but may be black, dark gray or reddish. It can be formed almost totally from the shells and bones of sea creatures, and fossils are often found in it. Some limestone can consist of whole coral reefs that have fossilized.

Limestone containing a variety of fossils

➡ CHALK

Chalk is a very fine-grained type of limestone, made up of the skeletons of tiny sea animals. Fossils of creatures such as sea urchins are often found in it. It is usually pure white, showing how clear the seas were when it was formed, but it can be stained brown or yellow. Chalk is usually porous, which means it absorbs liquid.

⬅ OOLITE

This limestone is made of tiny ball-shaped grains called ooliths. Grains of quartz sand and fragments of shell and other fossils may be among them. It is usually yellow to white, but can be brown or red. Ooliths are formed as layers of calcite build up around grains of sand that are being rolled along the seabed by the sea's currents.

SEDIMENTARY ROCKS

➡ STALACTITES and STALAGMITES

Both stalactites and stalagmites are found in limestone areas. Stalactites hang from the roofs of caves, while stalagmites grow up from the floor. They are formed when water containing dissolved calcite drips down, leaving a small amount of calcite behind.

Stalactite

Stalagmite

⬅ TRAVERTINE and TUFA

These are both formed from calcite dissolved in water. They contain lots of holes and cavities, so they look spongy. Both rocks can be reddish, white or yellow. Travertine is found around hot springs and geysers, while tufa occurs in limestone caves and around springs.

Travertine

For a link to a website with "geomysteries" to solve, turn to page 61.

➡ FLINT NODULES
Flint nodules (often just called flints) are made of chalcedony and form rounded lumps that separate easily from the rocks around them. They are often found in chalk, and are usually white on the outside and black inside. Flints are often the size of a potato but can be much bigger. They may be spherical or sausage-shaped.

⬅ PYRITE NODULES
These nodules are made of the mineral pyrite. They are found in sedimentary rocks, such as chalk, siltstone and shale. The nodules are made up from long, thin pyrite crystals, which radiate outward from the middle of the nodule. They are brown or black outside, with a shining yellow inside.

SEDIMENTARY ROCKS

➡ CONGLOMERATE
Conglomerate is made up of rounded fragments with a sandy material in between. It is formed from material washed down rivers and along coastlines. The fragments may be of any hard rock, and range in size from small pebbles to boulders. It varies in color, depending on the type of rocks that it is made up of.

⬅ BRECCIA
Breccia, like conglomerate, is made of fragments of rock held together by a finer sandy material. In breccia, the fragments are angular. This shows that they were not carried far by water, as this would have rounded them. Fragments vary from pebbles to boulders, and may consist of almost any type of rock.

METAMORPHIC ROCKS

➡ MARBLE

Marble is made mainly of the mineral calcite. It is a metamorphic rock formed by heat or pressure on limestone. It can be white, light brown or gray, but also black, green, or red. The word "marble" is sometimes used for other rocks, such as alabaster.

⬅ QUARTZITE

This is made mainly of grains of quartz, but it may contain feldspar, mica or other minerals, too. Quartzite is metamorphosed quartz sandstone. It has an even texture and the quartz grains are closely packed together. It is often white, but may be yellowish, gray or reddish.

METAMORPHIC ROCKS

➡ SLATE
Slate is formed by the metamorphism of shale and mudstone. It is made of tiny grains of minerals, such as mica, which are too small to be seen with the naked eye. It can be split easily into thin sheets, along surfaces known as cleavage planes. It may be black, red, greenish or purple.

⬅ PHYLLITE
Like slate, phyllite is made of metamorphosed shale and mudstone. Phyllite has been heated and squeezed more than slate, so the minerals it contains are coarser. Phyllite splits easily into sheets and slabs revealing a surface that is usually shiny. It is green to silver-gray in color.

For a link to a website with an interactive rock cycle, turn to page 61.

➡ MICA SCHIST

Schists are mainly metamorphosed siltstone and mudstone. Mica schist is composed mainly of mica (biotite or muscovite, or both) along with some quartz and feldspar. If it is made of muscovite, it tends to be silvery gray and sparkling. If it is mainly biotite, it may be brown or black.

⬅ GARNET SCHIST

This is like mica schist, but it also contains garnets. Garnets are often dark red, though they can be green or white. They are rounded in shape and vary in size. The rock splits easily due to the mica it contains. It occurs with other metamorphic rocks, such as mica schist, phyllite and amphibolite.

53

METAMORPHIC ROCKS

➡ AMPHIBOLITE

This is a medium- to coarse-grained rock made mostly of the mineral hornblende. Amphibolite is usually black or dark green and is often banded with dark and light layers. It is formed mainly from metamorphosed igneous rocks, such as basalt.

⬅ GNEISS

Gneiss is made mostly of feldspar, mica (biotite or muscovite) and quartz. The feldspar may form large pink or white crystals that look like eyes. Gneiss is often formed at a very high temperature – it may even partly melt. This results in dark and light layers that alternate in wavy, swirling folds.

For links to two online guides to rocks and minerals, turn to page 61.

FOSSILS

Fossilized leaves

◀ FOSSIL PLANTS

Fossil plants are usually found in fine-grained sedimentary rock, such as mudstone and shale. Some date from about 300 million years ago. Some of the best-preserved plant fossils are leaves and twigs, found in rocks formed between 65 and 1.8 million years ago.

Single fossil coral

➡ CORAL

Coral consists of simple animals with skeletons made of calcite. They are often preserved as fossils. Coral fossils may be single or in groups, called colonies. Fossils of animals that lived in the coral, such as gastropods and bivalves (see page 56), are often found with the coral.

A colony of fossilized coral

FOSSILS

➡ GASTROPODS

These are commonly known as snails. Their shells are usually coiled in spirals. Their fossils are found in shales, mudstones and limestones formed as far back as 540 million years ago.

Three different kinds of gastropods

Two different bivalves

⬅ BIVALVES

These include cockles, mussels and razor shells. Their shells are made of two separate parts, called valves, that are hinged together so the animals inside can open them up to feed and close them for protection. Their fossils are found in shales, limestones and mudstones.

➡ BRACHIOPODS

Like bivalves, brachiopods have a hinged pair of shells, but the two are a different size and shape, so that one overlaps the other. Their fossils are found in shales, limestones and mudstones, especially those formed between 500 and 285 million years ago.

Some brachiopods' shells have grooves and ridges.

⬅ ECHINOIDS (sea urchins)

These are rounded or heart-shaped animals up to 4 inches (100mm) across. The shell is made of plates of calcite, often covered with lumps. On modern-day sea urchins, spines are attached to these lumps, but the spines are rarely preserved in fossils. Echinoids are found in rocks, especially chalk, that were formed less than 200 million years ago.

Echinoid fossil with lumps, showing where the spines used to be

Heart-shaped echinoid fossil

A modern-day sea urchin with spines

57

FOSSILS

➡ AMMONITES

These were creatures which swam freely in the sea, buoyed up by air inside their shell. They are now extinct. Their fossils are flat spirals and are found in rocks formed 245 to 65 million years ago.

A living ammonite may have looked like this Nautilus, which is found in tropical seas today.

Belemnite fossils are often found broken.

A living belemnite may have looked like this.

⬅ BELEMNITES

Belemnites are extinct sea creatures that looked a little bit like squids. Belemnite fossils are the remains of part of their insides. They are bullet-shaped with a pointed end, and may vary in size, from the length and thickness of a match to 4 inches (10cm) long.

➡ TRILOBITES

Trilobites were sea creatures that appear in rocks that were formed between 500 to 300 million years ago. Their bodies consisted of a head, body segments and tail. It is the head and tail that are usually found as fossils. They are mainly found in siltstones and mudstones.

A complete trilobite may have looked like this.

The fossilized outlines of two trilobites

A shark's head showing the triangular teeth

⬅ FISH TEETH

Rays and sharks have soft bodies which do not fossilize well, but their teeth do. Most fossilized teeth are triangular, and are most commonly found in rocks formed between 65 and 144 million years ago.

USEFUL WORDS

abrasive – something rough that is used to smooth down other surfaces.

cavities – holes or hollows in solid rock.

cement – minerals that behave like glue, binding other minerals and rocks together.

cleavage – the direction in which some rocks and minerals split apart.

crust – a thin outer coating on a rock or mineral.

crystal – a naturally occurring solid substance with flat surfaces.

deposit – something that builds up gradually, which has been left behind by another substance, for example sediment carried in water.

element – one of the simple substances of which all matter is made. An element cannot be broken down into a simpler substance.

gemstone – a valuable mineral that is hard and rare, such as diamond.

geyser – a hole in the ground through which hot water and steam emerge.

iridescent – having different colors that shimmer and change according to the way you look at them.

mass – a lump of rock or mineral that does not have a definite shape.

massive – the word that describes a mass.

nodule – a rounded lump of mineral found in sedimentary rocks.

opaque – not letting light travel through; not transparent.

sediment – animal remains, and tiny fragments worn away from rock surfaces by rain, ice and wind.

translucent – allows light to travel through, but not clear, like glass.

transparent – easy to see through.

vein – a thin layer of rock or mineral between larger layers of a different rock or mineral.

INTERNET LINKS

If you have access to the Internet, you can visit these websites to find out more about rocks and minerals. For links to these sites, go to the Usborne Quicklinks Website at **www.usborne-quicklinks.com** and enter the keywords "spotters rocks".

Internet safety

When using the Internet, please follow the **Internet safety guidelines** shown on the Usborne Quicklinks Website.

WEBSITE 1 A huge interactive website packed with information on gems and minerals, with maps, close-up photos and slideshows.

WEBSITE 2 An online guide to rocks, minerals, fossils and geology, with useful advice on organizing a collection.

WEBSITE 3 Information on rock collecting equipment and how to store a rock collection.

WEBSITE 4 A fun introduction to Earth science, with lots of ideas for things to do.

WEBSITE 5 Games to test your mineral knowledge, and useful information on starting a collection.

WEBSITE 6 Find out more about rocks by solving some "geomysteries."

WEBSITE 7 Explore an interactive rock cycle.

WEBSITE 8 Find out more about the different periods of geologic time.

WEBSITES 9–10 Two more online guides to rocks and minerals.

SCORECARD

The rocks and minerals on this scorecard are in alphabetical order. When you spot one, fill in the date beside its name. A common one scores 5, a rare one is worth 25.

At the end of a day's spotting, add up all the points you have scored on a sheet of paper and keep a record of them. See if you can you score more points another day.

Name of rock or mineral	Score	Date spotted	Name of rock or mineral	Score	Date spotted
Agate	15		Chalcopyrite	20	
Agglomerate	25		Chalk	15	
Amethyst	20		Conglomerate	20	
Ammonites	15		Coral	20	
Amphibolite	25		Corundum	15	
Apatite	20		Crystalline calcite	10	
Aquamarine	10		Diamond	10	
Arsenopyrite	25		Dogstooth calcite	15	
Augite	20		Echinoids	20	
Barite	25		Emerald	10	
Basalt	15		Fish teeth	25	
Belemnites	20		Flint nodules	10	
Beryl	20		Fluorite	15	
Biotite	15		Fossil plants	20	
Bivalves	15		Gabbro	25	
Brachiopods	15		Galena	20	
Breccia	25		Garnet	10	
Carnelian	20		Garnet schist	25	
Chalcedony	25		Gastropods	20	

Name of rock or mineral	Score	Date spotted	Name of rock or mineral	Score	Date spotted
Gneiss	20		Pumice	25	
Goethite	25		Pyrite	15	
Gold	5		Pyrite nodules	15	
Granite	15		Pyrolusite	25	
Graphite	5		Quartzite	20	
Grit	10		Rhyolite	20	
Gypsum	15		Rock crystal	15	
Halite	5		Ruby	10	
Hematite	15		Sandstone	10	
Hornblende	20		Sapphire	10	
Limestone	15		Serpentine	15	
Magnetite	20		Serpentinite	20	
Malachite	20		Siltstone	15	
Marble	10		Silver	5	
Mica schist	20		Slate	5	
Milky quartz	10		Smithsonite	25	
Mudstone & Shale	10		Smoky quartz	25	
Muscovite	15		Sphalerite	20	
Obsidian	25		Stalactites & Stalagmites	25	
Olivine	20		Sulfur	15	
Oolite	25		Talc	10	
Opal	15		Tourmaline	20	
Orthoclase feldspar	15		Travertine & Tufa	25	
Pegmatite	25		Trilobites	25	
Phyllite	20		Tuff	20	
Plagioclase feldspar	15		Turquoise	15	

INDEX